The Eventful Flash

Bringing

Solar Waves of Change

Cheryl Lunar Wind and Friends

The Eventful Flash

Bringing Solar Waves of Change

Any Inquiries contact:

cheryl.hiller@yahoo.com

Some of the poems in this collection first appeared in Know Your Way, Follow the White Rabbit, Love Your Light, Life: Shared thru Poetry, Come to Mount Shasta, We Are Light, Finding Our Way Home, Star Messages, Grand Rising and Bloom Like Nature chapbooks; and on facebook.

Front cover photo credit, Mikasa Tamara Blue Ray

First edition.

Published by Alexander Agency Books, Mount Shasta, California 96067

ISBN 979-8-9897287-7-0

The Eventful Flash

Bringing

Solar Waves of Change

Preface

I was told to consider this year like a day.

"A day for a year."--Bible quote

At the beginning of this calendar year, I was
given the message---

'Grand Rising: A New Day Has Dawned' which
became the theme of my first book collection for
this year 2024.

Now here we are mid year, in the heat of summer,
Solstice--and the message I received recently has
become the subject for this new collection of poetry
and messages;

'The Eventful Flash: Bringing Solar Waves of Change'.

All of creation; Plant, Animal, Human, Angelic & Elemental
kingdoms are working in tandem during this Grand shift
supporting one another.

(Dragon helpers are especially active with their fiery energy.)

By acknowledging the loving support of other beings we unite
in this beautiful collaboration called Ascension.

Things are really heating up! What's gonna be next?

"Perceive Light in things, and Experience its Reflection.
You will see how power-filled you are.
All is truly well indeed."
--Eric Darnell

Contents

Cosmic Bells are Ringing
by Mikasa Tamara Blue Ray

It is time to sound the Bells
The Blue Bells blessed times Foretells
Hear the Divine Sound Ringing
Heaven with Us is Singing
With help of Ashtar Fleet
The transmission is Complete
Galactic energy in Action
Guaranteed Satisfaction
Heart Intelligence is One of a Kind
Wiser than the Way of the Mind
Only Divine Love Flow
Passes through Mother's Bow
The Blue Rays deleted all the Spells
It is time to sound the Bells

Solar Flash
by Cheryl

The moon winks,
dozes, Zzzzz
while planets
swirl in orbit.
Our Sol Star
glowing Super
Nova.

The flora and fauna
will swoon--
sway,
when the Daystar
makes its
appearance.

The Solar wind brings us
Gift packages,
a sonic shower
of protons, electrons--
Coronal Stream.

This is
the Event--
Grand Solar Flash.

the event
by Cheryl

I want to tell you about a gathering.

It is a Cosmic happening.

Some call it the Event.
It has been planned long in advance.

All are invited----
the ancients, the innocents---even those viewed
as guilty.

Our acceptance gives us admittance.
Our knowing is the ticket.
The practice of peace will be our map.

The Cosmic Rays show us the way,   a cipher,
they light up the path.

Sacred codes are hidden like Easter eggs.
We find them all over---
In nature, on our clocks and in our dreams.
We create them in music and art.

Our family are waiting for us---
they hail from far and near.
The sacred Earth clans are present---
tree, crystal, bird, wolf, bear and deer tribes,
AND
Those who have traveled a millennium to be present.
All are here---

The Divine Director pulls the curtain,
It is a beautiful scene,
Glorious light fills the room.

Children of the Sun
by Cheryl

The god of ale
came to me and said
'take a whiff'
'have a sip'

You are a winner--
take a bow--
claim your prize--
a trip to the dome.

The dome shines, sparkles--
a golden Sun god.
Sura.

Children of the Sun---
Open your eyes
and see,
a secret message.

The Horizon---
holds the Key--
secrets lay
between the lines
spaces
ley lines--

Stepping
on earth grids,
We ignite the way
sparkle and shine
for all to see--
like a vein of gold
rising to the surface
hot lava
streaming---forging
new trails.

Portal by Cheryl

Feeling gratitude and awe
for this next step.
We are on the cusp
of a Big Leap.

Who else feels it?
The excitement is in the knowing.
We have made it.
Give thanks to all your helpers.

I'm like a child's balloon filled with helium---
that needs held onto.
Catch it
Or,
let go--
Fly.

We are one of the many threads
in this tapestry of life.

Slip thru the eye
of the needle.
Come out on the other side.
Portal.

Love Letter from Spirit
by Yvonne Trafton

Green web
Web of green
Green Ribbons
Ribbons of Green
Green DNA Strands
Strands of DNA
My Strands
Spinning Strands
Sacred Geometry In Motion
Motion in geometry
Poetry in motion
to my delight
Ribbons of Delight
alit, alit
they light, they light
light up
blue strands,
gold strands,
white strands,
green strands
rose light
violet light
activate
activation, activation.
Iam Activated
My DNA Activated
alit Iam
Iam alit
light Iam
Iam Light
Bright Iam
Iam Bright
bright, bright, bright
so bright.

Heart bright, heart bright
bright heart
heart alit, heart alit
heart of light, heart of light
heart light

green heart
heart of green
green light, green light
light of mine
my light, my light
green light.

WE smile, we smile
Heart shinning brightly
We smile, we smile
She's alit
Yvonne's alit
We smile, we smile
heart light, heart shine
shine she will
she wills
we smile
shine she will
shinny smiles
we will
all's well
heart wells
our swells.

Rejoicing, rejoicing
Rejoice
Rejoice in Self
Self Rejoicing
We rejoice
In voice, in-fold
Enfolding
Light revelings
Beauty unfoldings
Unfold onto thee
Ode onto thee.
Dancing heart
Heart a' dancing
WE ARE DANCING
WE ARE REJOICING
HEART REJOICINGS
LOVE LETTER ONTO THEE
You are loved, you are love,
heart of love,
green love, green light, green heart.
7

Sunbursts of love
love as strong as the sun
you are the sun
sun brights, bright as sun
you are not alone
you are surrounded in love
you are love
loving you
in love with you
loving me, loving me
in love with me.

Heart activations
Heart callings
Call of the heart
Heart callings
Heart of ONE
the one, the one.
HON
Hum-ON
Just hum.

LOVE YOU ~

I Am by Cheryl

In the cosmos, I am
a Solar Quartz--
shimmering, sparkling.

My blinding starlight
brings healing, love and
synchronicity.

I shine mauve, orange and
lavender-- all at once.

I smell like cinnamon and
sassafras tea.

I run like a black equine---
Secretariat.

I hobnob my way to write
poetry at the cattywampus!

What is Personal Satisfaction?
by Le'Vell Zimmerman

You are not responsible for another souls emotional state beloved.

We all get to choose how to feel or respond to our experience as Creator Beings.

Personal satisfaction is the individual soul's responsibility in having the gift of Free will.

Healing within is where you evolve beyond all forms of external dependency, which includes emotional dependency on others to feel whole.

"Relationships" serve you in many ways, to include expanding upon the gratitude you already have within for the gift of being alive.

Ironically, it is your own capacity of personal satisfaction that is the most "attractive" state of being here within this hologram.

Reflect.

Self Love is the foundation of all Love.

-333

Growth is found
by Pradeep Nawarathna (pcnawarathna@gmail.com)

Silence is loud,
Stillness is vast.
In quiet and calm,
Life's cast.
No noise, no haste,
Growth is found.
In silence, in still,
Peace is crowned.

Stress, a teacher
by Pradeep Nawarathna

Breathe in peace, let worries cease,
Mind's eye open, heart's release.
Stress may come, but we'll be wise,
Mindful moments, our heart's prize.
With each breath, we find our core,
Stress teaches, we grow more.
Grateful for the lessons given,
Mindful living, stress forgiven.

Self Care Brings Mercy
by Susan Grace

You want to feel better.
Keep it simple.
There's no need for emo drama.
Just be honest.

The unknown doesn't have a qualitative charge.
It's not good or bad.
It's You and Life continually meeting in the
unfolding.

We get caught up in insecurity, escape, avoidance,
When disappointment and fear of repeating patterns
takes over.

So don't let it.

Self care brings mercy to the current moment.
You are safe here.

Be willing to experiment and shift your perspective.

We heal our way higher.
We do it together.

--XO

Limitations
by Le'Vell Zimmerman

Know that your "expectations" are all limited
beloved.

It would be wise to let them go...

You are here to experience great blessings that
you could never imagine.

The emotional content of your visualizations is
helpful in that they cater to the feelings of joy and
excitement within you that is elevating your
frequency, however how your path will unfold is
beyond all logical comprehension and that which
you can imagine at present.

Once again, your expectations lead to disappointment,
where it remains with your healing process that you
let go in knowing that you wrote this story before
you were born into your current physical vehicle.

You have the ability to "add to" your current story
through your imaginative and emotional faculties,
however to feel as if you need to "positively think
up a great life for yourself" right now here is clearly
an error in consciousness.

This has always been your story beloved.

There have never been any mistakes, accidents, or
coincidences here within this orchestration of
Infinite Intelligence.

Your spiritual maturity is in healing yourself enough
beyond the voice in your head to allow a return home
to your Heart Space in working with your experience
as The Creator and author of this now moment.

-3333

Excavations by Cheryl

What gifts do you have buried?

Go in that cave--
deep down, clean it out.

The deeper you dive
the higher you'll fly.

Come fly with me---
fold time and space.

Dive into the sun--
Go there,
this now moment--
Fly free.

Fly Free by Cheryl

Round and Round
We go---

swirl, whirl, twirl

Take your turn.

I am the marble in the Roulette wheel---
Circling.

I am a pebble in the whirlpool.

Take your turn.

Turn dirt into pearls.

I Am a pearl.

Go thru the furnace---come out,
all shiny and new---
Phoenix.

Fly Free--
unencumbered by others ideas, expectations, demands.

What's Happening
by Cheryl

Every once in a while
you just have to fall apart----
When you pick yourself up, and
put the pieces back together,
you become a different picture.

Falling apart
is something
that
happens often
for me---
lately.
Like every
other day.

The in between
days---
are
for re-assembly,
construction.

In Jenga,
the goal
is the collapse---

We collapse---
to regroup, remake,
revisit---
the who we are
becoming.

The fall---humanity has fallen---
And it was a choice.

How we go back together---
is also a choice.

Ashes, Ashes
We all fall down.

16

We are
the phoenix rising
out of the ashes.

Do not fear the falling,
do not fight it---
It is necessary.

Necessary evil?
We may not understand it---
want it or choose it---
But it is not evil,
just another stage
in the cycle
of evolution.

For growth
there must be
change,
shattered, broken open---
parts and pieces.

Then the building
can happen---
will happen---
The happening.

Maturing is a free will choice
by Le'Vell Zimmerman

Let them beloved...

Allow.

Unconditional Love is your nature.

You get to choose what to give your precious manifestation energy or "attention" to.

All must experience their own energy to heal.

Maturing is a free will choice.

You are not here "to sell" anything.

Your focus is what is manifesting for you right now.

-3333

Conscious Decisions
by Le'Vell Zimmerman

Just know that whatever you are paying attention to is being "paid for" as a conscious decision within you as a Creator Being.

The nature of your investments will be returned.

Indiscriminately.

The Love is unconditional.

-3333

"Justice is letting go of the need to be right.
The ego wants to be right, always--
It is a tool that can become unbalanced.
Ever hear of a big head?
You can keep it in check--by asking
What does this thought serve?"
---Cheryl Lunar Wind

A Message by Cheryl

Every day is a different reality---
Yesterday's events
matter not.

It's all a hologram anyway--
So you don't need to be concerned--
Try to fix anyone--

Tomorrow
we'll all be awash
in an ocean
of sunlight.

Just be kind,
the rest will work itself out.

epigee (apogee)
by Cheryl

I am a bud, gradually gently opening.

Nothing will come to pass
if it doesn't receive your energy.

Illusions dissipate without our(creator) energy.

"You are generating this hologram beloved,"

It doesn't matter
What
they are doing.

Just
Walk away--
Like
An epigee of awareness--
You can
love all from a distance.

Mirage **by Cheryl**

The way home---

I think about a shortcut---
a way out of this reality.

The only way out
is through it.

When I was pregnant
and it was getting close to my time,
I was terrified of delivery--
but I told myself
the only way out
is through it.

A sleepless night---
the only way out
is through it.

You can't mourn
what you never had---
It's all a mirage--
a hologram.

Friendships, arrangements, deals--
all part of the hologram.

It's ok to be sad
by Cody Ray Richardson

I'm glad to be sad
Sad means I can feel
Sad means I'm not mad
Not being mad means I'm facing the pain
I'm not running from the drag
Sad means I'm sober
Sad means I'm facing myself
 not rolling over
Sad means I'm still here
Sad means I'm looking myself in the mirror
I want to help people feel
As sad as it is
Sadness is real
It's ok to be sad
Life hurts bad
It's ok if your sad
I won't try to fix you this time
I accept it
I'm glad
Because you being sad
Means you are not mad
After all sadness is motivation for change
So someday it won't be so bad

Ground & Allow the Flow
by Le'Vell Zimmerman

No, you can't control what is happening in your life right now beloved...

But you do get to decide what happens next.

With grounding yourself more, you can truly "respond" from a place of great maturity versus "reacting" from a space of fear, pain, and ignorance, which only leads to more chaos on your path.

With a more balanced presence within there is more emotional maturity and self governance as a Creator Being.

Whoever controls your emotions, controls you life...

Only through "grounding yourself" are you consciously present enough to decide for yourself how to feel right now in not allowing others to emotionally manipulate you.

No, this is not about "controlling your emotions", but allowing them to flow through you naturally and being present enough to simply observe them and decide which emotions you prefer to entertain more.

-3333

Shadows/Cycle of Life
by JahSun

You won't see the shadows when we glow
Light shines down from above
Submit yourself to the flow
And brace yourselves
For Love

Struggle comes, and then it goes
Love is the song we all know
Stars shine bright, then they die
Such is the cycle of life

Send your prayers up to the sky
And to this Earth may she alight
A burning fire in your Soul
To return, to return us all Home

Look at the Sun/Change Within
by JahSun

Look at the sun begin to rise
Over the green rolling hills I'm lucky to be alive

Feel the warmth beat down unto my eyes
As the dark turns to day see the colors by my side

> And I feel, something happening
> Yes I feel, a change within

See the sun in the sky
And watch the birds as they fly by
See the light shining through the trees
As I sit back and wonder, what it means to me

> And I feel, something happening
> Yes I feel, a change within

Watch the sun in the west
Its been a long hard day and I've tried to do my best
See the sun sinking low
Beneath the watery waves tells me its my time to go

> Still I feel, something happening
> Yes I feel, a change within

Becoming Light
by Cody Ray Richardson

As you rise in spiritual consciousness
You will disconnect from worldly matters
With your view being higher
You will see more darkness around you
Becoming light means you will feel separate
Because you are
This world is impermanence
You are forever
The closed loop system of this world is not you
While some fight for a grain
You know to plant it
The only fight you win is the one you are not in
All times exist at once
Thought proceeds matter
Your thoughts matter
Separate what is yours from what is not
This separation feeds clarity
A clear mind is a calm mind
A calm mind is a clear view
A clear view shows a way
A way in which you can navigate

Fairy
by Amala Amunet

They say I'm too airy fairy
Come back to earth
Be realistic
This is how you should work and measure your worth
But what is realistic?
A socially acceptable habitual behavior?
Is this the law of absolute truth?
Or a momentary fluke of limitation
No thank you my friend
Because how I see it I was born with wings
And I hid them too long in this societal conditioning
I'm deprogramming, reprogramming
These light codes eternal vibration raising my frequency
This is my reality
I earned these wings
I'll illuminate, elevate, and transcend to a bliss state
These wings of innocence and purity
Heralding a wave of hope
Birthing a new earth
An ancient heaven
Our destiny
So, no thank you my friend
I see the ineffable majesty within
I fly free,
While walking this plane
And airy fairy I shall remain

Compassion
by Pradeep Nawarathna (pcnawarathna@gmail.com)

In the quiet of our hearts,
Where compassion takes its stand,
We find the truth that binds us all,
Life's fragile thread in hand.

For every act of violence,
A ripple through the soul,
We pause to see the other's pain,
And choose a different role.

To walk in shoes not our own,
To feel their joys and strife,
Is to embrace our shared humanity,
And honour every life.

So let us be the change we seek,
In kindness, love, and grace,
For when we lift each other up,
We find our rightful place.

Freedom Blooms Within
by Pradeep Nawarathna

Release anger's grip, let pride subside,
Detach from all, let attachments slide,
Mind and body unclung, sorrow denied,
Freedom blooms within, like morning tide.

The Tale of the Two-Headed Bird
by Pradeep Nawarathna (pcnawarathna@gmail.com)

In Himalayan heights, a curious bird soared,
Two heads, one body—a marvel to behold.
One head, eyes aflame with envy's fire,
 The other, savoring sweetness, higher.

The Jealous Gaze One head watched, seething,
as the other dined,
Sweet fruit's nectar on its beak entwined.
"Why not me?" whispered Envy's cruel plea,
"Let poison fill my veins; then both shall see."

The Bitter Choice The envious head, heedless
of fate's decree,
Chose poison's kiss—a bitter symphony.
The bird convulsed, wings fluttering in strife,
Two minds, one body, now entwined in afterlife.

 Lessons Carved in Feathers And so,
dear wanderer, heed this tale:
 Envy's venom devours, hearts frail.
Two heads, one choice—a cautionary song,
Seek not to harm, but soar where virtues throng.

For envy's fruit, once tasted, leaves no flight,
Only echoes of wings lost in eternal night.
Moral Lesson: Choose Unity Over Discord

The bird's dual heads symbolize our inner conflicts—
our desires and jealousies.
Envy led one head to consume poison, resulting
in the bird's demise.
The lesson: When we allow discord within ourselves,
we harm our own well-being.
Choose unity, compassion, and balance;
let both heads row towards shared purpose.

May our hearts choose sweetness over poison,
and may our wings carry us towards compassion.

29

Red & Gold Dragon Guardian
by Cheryl

A red and gold lizard
came to me--
he said
    "Take a toke. Majik dust--
    Drink the gold. Spice up your life."

and shared
    "I used to be a fish stuck in a pond."

Take it up a notch.
Move up the scale--
Bass, Alto or Soprano?
What tone are you?

Stretch
    a little higher.
Stuck?

Rock that boat--
gently, calmly. It's safe.
Make your move--

Change.

Red Rose Dragon
by Cheryl

Water dragons live in the sea--
Air dragons hide in the clouds--
Land dragons are in nature--
places like gardens, forests and mountains.

They love the flowers, playing hide and seek with them.

Some male, some female--
they visit Earth like a field trip. (trip to the park)

I have a special dragon friend, her name is Red Rose.
She shape shifts from dragon to rose and back again.

Don't go looking for a dragon, for
they won't be found.

Wait,
and they will come to you.

Arcturian Message
from Lauren Willow Fox

Open to the light
The light is you
Solar star power
Starlight
Renew

Sunshine is you
Shadows dissolving
Earth revolving
All evolving
Held in glorious light

God is love
Christ Sun consciousness
Love is you
Hold each other
Sister and brother

Love Your Light
by Cheryl

The Sun is the heart
of all that is.

Our heart is a Sun--
shining, sparkling
lighting our path.

We Are the Key
by Cheryl

The Event
is not based on the external--
<u>what</u> or <u>when</u>
will the Sun bring it.

When we reach
the level of awareness,
a certain frequency
that will trigger
the Event.

We carry the codes,
that just need switched on--
Enough of those 'lights' being
turned on--
tell Mother Earth, Father Sun and
all the universal family
that we are ready.

We Are the Key.

The Eventful Flash
by Cheryl

the event
the flash
Full of light
Flashing Flares and light codes...Galore

eruptions, itching
on my chest
like filaments
bursting from the sun

Record breaking flares--
a tidal wave, washing
over us.

A photonic ocean,
white, light
engulfing
encompassing Earth--
surrounding
holding her--
for better or worse;

the waves of light
are
changing
all they
come in contact with.

Purposeful.
Eventful.
Evolution.

True Self
by Le'Vell Zimmerman

You are not the Ego Minds endless list of
temporary "opinions" beloved.

You are the eternal silence that observes them
unconditionally.

The true self doesn't have an opinion.
Your soul's preferences remains within its
harmonic essence that materializes naturally with
presence beyond dependency on verbalization.

Masters know.

33:33

The Return
by Jimi Reddick

The Father approaches the Son
My child, what have you done?
Twas only a fraction of our endless time
I left to you a task tending this garden of mine
Now I return and Oh what a mess,
The flowers are smoking and
The monkey is wearing a dress

The fish are coughing and
The birds only rap without song
It's a beautiful mess, definitely gone wrong.

I'll ask of you to return down the hill
Please clean up the mess
So as to avoid the till
We've done this before and now it's come so far
It would be a shame to reset
All that We are

Hesitantly examining the scars on his wrists
With Still aching shoulders, and wide open fists
He offers his Father a view of his crown,
a thorny reminder of the last time he went down...

Daddy, you remember what happened before?
I did my best and yet they chose to ignore
Blaming ME for their ignorance and doing their best
At the worst things possible
So hear my request...

I will do ask you ask
And I shall return
I only ask you to be with me
So that you can learn
How some of the creatures in your garden don't care
I told them the truth
And that's my cross to bear.
Please watch over as this task I accept
Scars last forever the pain diminished the more I wept.

Son I am with you always and I do recall
Your example of inspiration to
All creatures great and small
No harm shall befall you as
You have proven your love
 Only evil shall be burned
As I observe from above

Now do as you promised
And let it be known
My Son has returned to the garden we've sown
Hear this little flowers, animals still learning
Examine your self when you feel that burning
Your soul lives forever
But your Earthly life you may lose
It's all up to you

Which path do you choose?

What Is Right?
by Cheryl

If you think you know something, what is right
...just know that you do.

We all know our right path based on our free
will choices. We base our decisions on our
 hearts' desire and past experiences.
So how can anyone else decide for others?

This is a violation of the Universal law of
Free Will
and falls in the realm of judgment.

It is really ugly when people elevate themselves
above others because they disagree with their
free will choices....examples are many....such
as choice of food or drink....whether to smoke
this or that.

Regardless of the health benefits of these paths
please be aware of the divisive nature of judgment.

Practice the art of allowing and
your sharing will be with kindness.

We Don't Need Rescued
by Le'Vell Zimmerman

No one is here to "rescue you" beloved.

You are here to liberate yourself.

Reclaiming your own sovereignty via this opportunity to awaken beyond the programs of "separation" is a choice, where feeling there is a force outside of you "to fight" only continues to validate these programs based in division amongst this hologram.

"Fighting" remains a self destructive symptom of insanity amongst the unawakened within the illusion of Duality beloved.

You are not here to "play anybody's games".

Creator Beings acknowledge the catalyst of the illusion, however make their own decisions to validate and participate or not.

Peace remains the eternal truth.

All else is temporary.

-3333

July Energy Update: Spreading Light
by Shivrael

What is the energy like this month?
Right now at the beginning of July, we are
experiencing a ramping up of energy. There is a
feeling of impending change just around the
corner. Empaths and intuitive people feel
apprehension about the unknown that is to come.

Peaks

The Akashic records speak in images. I see an
image of a ramp going toward a peak. What does this mean?
The meaning is that we are entering a time of
"peak chaos." Simultaneously, we are also entering
a peak of spiritual energies. The spiritual energies
can feel peaceful and joyful and also overwhelming.

The Bigger Picture is Beautiful

What else can we expect? The landscape gets
clearer. Imagine that you are at a vista point
looking out at the landscape around you and
below you. You can focus on what you don't like
or see the overall view from the peak. From the
bigger picture, all is beautiful and all is well.
Take the long view that all is falling into place
in your life and the greater whole. Trust the outcome.
Who you are at the beginning of July will be different
than who you are in the middle of August. How will
that be? I see the lenses of the eyes have a cloudy
film covering that gets removed. You will see yourself
and the world around you more clearly at that time.
Everything comes into focus.

Sorting, Cleansing, Purging and Releasing

The next image from the Akashic Library is of sorting.
In the image, hands are throwing tablets (representing
records of the past) into two different piles. You can see
one pile as old 3D stuff and the other as what you wish
to take to 5D. It is a time of letting go of old records,

beliefs, stories, and emotional patterns; anything that is not serving you- let it go. The universe wants to release the past. Find yourself cleansing and purging, creating simplicity, a calmer mind, and a greater ability to be present in the now.

A reminder is to place your bare feet on the Earth in nature, which restores the spirit. Allow yourself to slow down and reset to a calmer place, with less complexity. Experience and cultivate a more organic direct connection with Mother Earth. Your tools are prayer, meditation, contemplation, and gratitude while honoring the divine in all beings and nature.

Meanwhile, there is a dynamic, fast-moving, energetic, combustible, energy of fire that purges the old. You might experience or witness heat and feel irritable. You may be challenged to stay grounded and calm on some days when the cosmic energies are strong.

Spreading Light

July's energy shows so many lit candles over a map of the USA and the other nations. Each person is holding a candle and they are connected with light. This indicates more awakening, more light than ever. It is as if the candle of one is passed on to another, friend to friend. The light activates one person to the next person with a new frequency and awareness of reality.

A message is that our sight is getting clearer like rose-colored glasses are being removed. It is a time to see what is real under the surface. In this coming time, you may be able to face what you might not have allowed yourself to in the past. Facing reality might feel like "tough love from the universe."
What does that mean? You are called to step up from consuming and being a consumer. You are called to know yourself beyond a body, as a spiritual being. Question all that holds you back to shining your highest and greatest light in the world.
Step into being a spiritual being beyond being a human being. The energies of compassion and caring are activated as you see the greater whole that you are (with everyone included.)
There may be more chaos and craziness in the world. July may have more ups and downs emotionally unless you look within. Ride the wave with the energy of chaos with equanimity, on the vista peak witnessing and watching it all play out.

41

"Be of the world but not in it" when feeling overwhelmed.

Ask yourself, when sucked into some sort of drama---
"Is this for me?" Am I a witness or a character in the play?
Return to witness consciousness, staying out of other people's business.

How do we best navigate the energies of July?

With a surfboard (laughter from Spirit, with a wink).
What might that mean? To find your balance as you surf big waves of emotional energy that is not yours but in your field. Cool the heat, passion, intensity, and chaos of July with play and being in the water. Let yourself ride the best wave with perfect timing. The ideal timing comes from trusting your heart to know when to surf and ride, and when to let a wave pass by. Let yourself float over the top. The surface of the ocean has waves which can be seen as emotional upsets. You can choose to know that you are the entire ocean or you may identify with one ripple of emotion. If you do so, you may miss the wave that was meant for you. Let your body float over the waves of emotions, awaiting the perfect ride to shore.

The next image is of picking fruit. Choose what is ripe, what is ready for harvest, and what appeals to you most. Find the sweetness in life. Consume (thoughts, emotions, news, food, substances) that nourish your physical and emotional bodies. The rose-colored glasses coming off forces you to look at yourself and your habits (and maybe addictions.) You are invited to love yourself enough to notice what is toxic and what is nourishing. Always choose what nourishes your body, mind, and spirit.

Another way of seeing this idea- you are invited to pick fruit ripe for harvest, the most delicious available. This allows you to create a life by choosing the highest and best for yourself (which also benefits others.) In this fashion, you land on the highest timeline. You live as your highest potential self, igniting awareness in others, and finding your highest joy in the life that is meant for you.

May it be so,
Shivrael
Akashic Intuitive

The Final Song
by Cheryl

Say yes to music.

Chant, Drum, Dance.
Chant the words that you know.
You carry the song in your hearts.
Connect with the original beat.

Do you hear the cosmic tone?
The Bell is ringing.
Join the Universal Ohm.

Become Free.
Know Yourself.
Share your freedom.

Carry that feeling where ever you go.
Hear the final tune.
Be a clear vessel
and
Radiate the song
of
Love, Light and Peace.

There is a calling.
A Last call.
The Final Song.

The Final song is playing.
Listen.
The birds are singing
the Final Song.
One last chance---
to make a stand.

Stand up for right.
Be a protector---
        of the children, of the animals,
        of all Earth's inhabitants.
Be a guardian.

Stretch out your hand---
help a brother in need. *

Use your energy
to bless all life.
Pay it forward.
Pay with your Ka.
Live. Love. Give.

*Let's dance
one last dance.
It's the last dance,
last dance for love. ***

* Bill Withers, Lean on Me, 1972.
* Donna Summer, Last Dance, 1978.

<u>Many thanks to these contributors:</u>

Amala Amunet

Mikasa Tamara Blue Ray

Lauren Willow Fox

Susan Grace

Pradeep Nawarathna (pcnawrathna@gmail.com)

Jimi Reddik

Cody Ray Richardson

Shivrael

Jah Sun

Yvonne Trafton

Le'Vell Zimmerman

Author page--

Cheryl Lunar Wind lives in the Mount Shasta area in a little town called Weed. She is a practicer of Mayan cosmology, Lakota ceremony, Star Knowledge and the Universal Laws including the Law of One. Her hobbies are writing poetry, music, dance, drum circles and love for all life; plant, animal and crystal. Cheryl has been a guide and spiritual teacher for many years. Now she shares wit and wisdom through poetry, and has published poetry books; Know Your Way, We Are One, Follow the White Rabbit, Love Your Light, LIFE: Shared thru Poetry, Come to Mount Shasta: Sacred Path Poetry, We Are Light, Finding Our Way Home, We Are Forever, Handshake With the Divine, Grand Rising: A New Day Has Dawned, Star Messages: Codes to Sing, Dance and Live by, Return to Innocence, Bloom Like Nature: Live the Natural Way, Creativity Brings Peace: Create & Share Your Gifts, May Love Lead: Poetry for Living, Loving & Giving and The Eventful Flash: Bringing Solar Waves of Change.

Testimonials---

"Cheryl's poetry is very inspiring--particularly the way she compares life with the forces of nature. There is a special element in her poems that opens my heart and fills my soul with divine possibilities."
Giovanna Taormina, Co-Founder, One Circle Foundation

"Cheryl's poems have helped me to uncover and honor my own hidden memories. The beauty of her spirit is evident in each tender, insightful passage."
Marguerite Lorimer, www.earthalive.com

"A rare collection filled with raw, courageous honesty. Thought provoking words that will stop you in your tracks."
Snow Thorner, ED Open Sky Gallery, Montague, California

"When wisdom, guidance, confirming comfort, ect. arrives to us humans--from beings with the perspective of other realms--it is a divine gift. Especially in the form of what we call poetry, and through a being with no agenda; Cheryl Lunar Wind simply shares what source gives her!"---Dragon Love (Thomas) Budde

Cheryl,
Greetings and Happy Monday to you my friend. I just wanted to share with you that every time I read 'Come to Mount Shasta', even now that I'm mentioning it I cry, I cannot help it, it is such a Divine message and so impeccable in its timing. I came up here for Spirit, you know I was called by Source and I live on the mountain and I just want to thank you. Your poem found me last summer at the headwaters during the Alien and Angels conference; and then I found your book sitting in the gazebo and I just can't stop, I love it! I love you, thank you.
---Jim

Cheryl,
Just want to thank you for your bringing me into the community at Shasta. What you are doing/did do is absolutely changing my life. You did it, you were instrumental in helping me set my true path. Spirit is moving and the more of us that listen and act the sooner the shift will be completed.
---Darrel

About Cheryl's poetry--
"You are dynamic! I have known no one who does so much so swiftly, and your writing touches my heart because it comes from your heart."
---The Durwood Show

"Your words are my words. I keep your book 'Know Your Way' on my nightstand. I read it at bedtime and morning."
---Karina Arroyo

"Cheryl's words work magic in my heart, stirring the wisdom that is buried so deeply within me---beautiful indeed!"
---Ellie Pfeiffer, founder of Ellie's Espresso & Bakery, Weed, CA

www.ingramcontent.com/pod-product-compliance
Lightning Source LLC
Chambersburg PA
CBHW060643280326
41933CB00012B/2131